Traveling, Traveling

poems by

Nadell Fishman

Finishing Line Press
Georgetown, Kentucky

Traveling, Traveling

Copyright © 2022 by Nadell Fishman
ISBN 979-8-88838-050-5 First Edition
All rights reserved under International and Pan-American Copyright Conventions. No part of this book may be reproduced in any manner whatsoever without written permission from the publisher, except in the case of brief quotations embodied in critical articles and reviews.

ACKNOWLEDGMENTS

Thank you to Literary North for publishing "Expressionism" as part of their online page, Ekphrasis, 2020; and to the Plant-Human Quarterly for publishing "Lady's Slipper" in its Fall 2021 Issue #2.

Publisher: Leah Huete de Maines
Editor: Christen Kincaid
Cover Art: Judith Stuart Boroson, www.judithstuart.com,
        Author/Photographer: ChoreoGraphics: Six Studies
Author Photo: Emma Norman
Cover Design: Elizabeth Maines McCleavy

Order online: www.finishinglinepress.com
        also available on amazon.com

Author inquiries and mail orders:
Finishing Line Press
P. O. Box 1626
Georgetown, Kentucky 40324
U. S. A.

Table of Contents

Traveling, Traveling

Traveling, Traveling 1
Girlhood 3
Ma's Stories 4
Ma Waits Tables 6
My Cantor Sings No More 8
Family History in the Chair 9
Teeth 10
Zio Is Italian for Uncle 11
Hats 13
Nothing Can Stop It 15
Two Hawks, Riverside Park 17
Micro-Adjustments 19
Travis is 45 21
The Body Never Lies 23
A Daughter's Story 24
Happy Marriage I 25
                II 26
                III 27
Elegy I 29
Saturday Night at David's or the Right Tool for the Job 31
Was His 32
The Message 33
The #1 Train 34
Poetry in Motion 35
What Comes After the Middle Ages? 37
Elegy II 38
Letter in Which Love Is Invoked 40

Taking Off from Charles de Gaulle

Taking Off from Charles de Gaulle 45
An Annual Walk 46
Faire la Cuisine 48
Homage 49
Haricots Verts, Belle Mère 50
Expressionism 52
Synagogues 54
Swan Bar 57
Montparnasse Cemetery 59
Le Béguinage 60
Swans at Ouchy 62
Hvar Panorama 63
Taste, Memory 64
Voyage Out 66
Now & Then 67
Why She Falls 68
Moscow: Fear & Trembling 69
Road Trip 71

Coda

Lady's Slipper 75

Notes 77

for Bill Gazzola

Traveling, Traveling

Traveling, Traveling

There were those *Let's Get Lost* Sundays
in Dad's used clunkers, the *Olds* or the *Caddy*,
announcing to the neighborhood
our travels to distant realms—
Jersey or Westchester County—
and our late returns home
after dinners in diners
or the Catskills Chinese restaurant
owned by two old Yiddish-speaking women
kibitzing out back, refilling red and yellow
squeeze bottles with duck sauce and hot mustard.

At night, holding onto its sides,
I traveled on the ship of my mattress,
soaring through double windows
of the bedroom I shared
with my seven-years-older sister,
up through clouds, among the stars.
How else to fall asleep in a house of contradictions
where familial love between us
tangoed with silence that fogged us in?

Postcards arrived in the mail from rich relatives
who traveled exotically
to Miami Beach and *Disneyland*.
There was the fallen twig
from the family tree
that up and moved to Israel,
only to be swallowed up by the Dead Sea.
The Brooklyn triple-decker where
my Russian grandparents settled
with their baker's dozen of kids
and their wives, children, and husbands
was so close, we could hear each others' breaths.

But Mom and Dad would forever be
the pioneers of traveling,

traveling, as family legend would have it,
after they packed up their lives
in a few sorry suitcases
and turned their no longer youthful eyes from Brooklyn
to move with three kids to the hinterlands
of Queens, a hoard of relatives staring after them
from the border!

Girlhood

It was a 1960s *pencil skirt*
even before it had that name:
wool herringbone in beige and browns,
and it streamed from my skinny hips just past my knees,
a hand-me-down from my older cousins
to my older sister to me.

The tawny sweater too, with its one
pearlized button closure at the back,
beautiful on her voluptuous woman's body,
sagged on my flat frame.

That morning, when the elastic on my last pair
of clean underpants
felt stiff and worn but I pulled them up,
not knowing that they too
could be capable of treachery,

by the time I arrived at my Junior High,
those panties were beginning their mischief.
My two best friends shielded me from view,
as the band of elastic broke
and they began their descent: my panic
creeping up as they crept down.

I was fourteen and flat-chested.
Boys drew surfboards on the blackboards
obsessed with the ways my breasts failed me.

In tears at home, my mother told me:
those boys "played with me"
with their drawings and chants
because "they liked me" and woe,
wasn't that the moment
Treachery belched his putrid breath
over the future.

Ma's Stories

On September 17, 2010, Ma turned off her TV set
and with a long wobbly sigh, *"That's it, my stories are over, kaput!"*
Ma had been a cultish watcher of *As the World Turns*—

her *stories*—for 54 years. She knew
who slept with whose wife, who had whose illegitimate baby,
who had amnesia and how many times

and whose character died, but miraculously returned another season
with different hair, another storyline. Sometimes I'd watch
with her and to my amazement

life in Oakdale hadn't changed much in years.
The pace was slow and with soap bubble ads
that half-hour stretched satisfyingly on and on.

When I was little, before kindergarten wrenched me
from my loved ones and Ma started selling bridal gowns,
we'd pull up our tomato soup and grilled cheese on TV trays

and sometimes the beautiful stranger who came to do the ironing
sat with us and we'd be lost for 30 minutes in Proctor & Gambleland.
Then in 1967, like Dorothy stepping into Oz, the World

began turning in color, and eventually that was even true in our house
when the old black & white cathode finally burst its tube.
Something about the color was out of whack, though,

and the inhabitants of Oakdale suffered in a continuous state
of nausea, sour green tinting their edges.
But now it was over, a daytime desert for Ma's retirement.

These were her *stories*, she counted on them with the regularity
she couldn't get from her digestive system. Most importantly, the Hughes'
around which that world turned, were nothing like us.

They were doctors who ran a hospital and law partners in prestigious firms.
When they broke the law, honey, the law fixed itself ASAP.
You wouldn't catch matriarch Nancy without her strand of pearls

even elbow deep in a body cavity, she performed a classy surgery.
Then, as the end drew near, the writers bequeathed to Nancy a dignified death
in her sleep, the rest was the world turning small, smaller, and disappeared.

Ma Waits Tables

It's the first morning, and the first story
of her two-week visit.
We sit across from each other
in a faded maroon booth at the diner
on Broadway, a late breakfast.

The food comes wrong, twice:
how hard can it be, I whine, to remember
two orders of Eggs Florentine?
"This reminds me," she begins
as if a cue card's behind my head,

"I'm a girl of 17, working all the time,
I'm always tired. A friend of my father's
asks Pa for my help at his hotel weekends."
She'd never waited tables, she says,
and I realize,

I've never heard this story before
from my 93-year-old-mother.
"In those days in the Catskills
soup came in a mug, you poured it
into the soup bowl at the table, very fancy.

The owner's rabbi sits down with his family
and I wait on them. Wouldn't you know
he orders the soup, it's very hot
and I begin to pour, but, like our waiter
who doesn't know to write down

two orders of the same eggs,
I'm not paying attention.
Next thing I know, I'm pouring hot soup
into the rabbi's lap."
She leans in,

grows taller in the seat.
"I bust out laughing,
Yeah," she says,
my face incredulous
her face round and bright as a girl's.

"I'm too stupid to be afraid, she adds,
and everyone at the table busts out laughing.
They can't help it, even the rabbi
whose lap is filled with hot soup.
The owner is furious with me, turns red in the face

and tells my father. What happened, Pa asks?
It's too much, I say, I can't work so much. Okay, he says, stop."
The eggs finally arrive, and she eats with gusto
and relief as though she's been on her feet all day
and she can't get over how funny it all was.

My Cantor Sings No More

There were all the nights of noise
and through-the-looking-glass
confusions of sleep
that childhood could not surmount
and you, stalwart sentinel of my dreams—
my tall broad-shouldered dad—
you were the definition
of comfort because when I woke
whatever the dream or nightmare
it was replaced by your living self.
There was always more of you.
The singing, talking, laughing man,
you were sentient, larger than life—
two of my girl fingers
fit into your wedding ring.
Now, time is moving
the living you into the past
and in waking there is nothing
to replace that image, that sound.
Sound fades, is not infinite as light
that reports back in waves to earth
from billions of galaxies
time after time.
Your voice chanting: *l'dor va'dor*
from generation to generation
will not be heard again.
Memory's paltry engine
could keep you here:
that is one definition of nightmare.
Nothing will return you
to the world.

Family History in the Chair

The contours of a plastic covered dental chair
and the contours of a female body are not congruent,
leaving a gap between the small of my back
and its intended support.

My grandfather never sat in a dentist's chair
in Minsk. He was 65 when his teeth began to ache
in New York and he could no longer crack his beloved
pine nuts to freshen his breath.

The hygienist is a thorough and trustworthy woman
who talks to me without expecting answers.
The air amplifies her scraping sounds in the Operatory.
She knows my mouth better than I do.

Her copious notes remind her
of my high level of sensitivity
to this particular work environment,
but the unfamiliar dentist, he's another sort.

His job is to poke around, to try and dislodge
my ancient silver fillings, his predecessors' shoddy work.
I don't trust him. For a moment he hesitates—
a pointy probe hovering in one hand,

tiny mirror in the other. Through my bared teeth,
I swallow and growl as if to bite:
"Just so you know, my grandfather
dropped dead in a dentist chair when he was 65."

Teeth

Haven't you been staring into the bathroom mirror
at a foamy open mouth full of toothpaste all your life,
or at least since you grew your milk teeth?
Then one morning as you rinse away bubbles,
you're looking into someone else's mouth!
Like so many of your body's mysteries of aging,
your teeth, hardest substance in your body,
shift and twizzle themselves into a new configuration,
no longer content to inhabit their own chambers.

You missed that glacial movement in their pockets,
cement grown soft, enamel yellowed.
Every visit to the hygienist reveals a little more root,
a little more sensitivity causing sweat
to gather in your armpits, run cold down your sides as you grip
the seat's leather armrests and contemplate your chest
slamming against the room's ceiling
from the shock of metal striking nerve.

Once straight white teeth gleamed from your smile,
guarding pink tongue and walls of inner cheek. Lately, you gaze
toward a future in which you are nostalgic for the thoughtless
crunch of a raw carrot
and back at the indignity to your father that last time
bent over the table as he struggled to eat without
his dentures because at 94, his gums had shrunk.

Zio Is Italian for Uncle

When you're a child who doesn't fit
into the size and shape of your own name,
Nadell, and can't understand it yourself or
explain it no matter who asks or how,
you yearn to be a Susie or a Barbie
even Mary, as unlikely as
Bubbeh's name was
in an orthodox family.

Uncle Jack's marriage—
Zio Giovanni, I might
have called him had I known,
he was Italian—
to Aunt Lily, exploded the family
into mourning,

Bubbeh and Zaydeh turned away,
shunning their fourth or maybe
she was their fifth daughter—one of seven,
ten children altogether, which is a huge family
for Jews—until Lily's body, nearly giving up,
landed her in the hospital
and they had to come
because it was written,
and Jack (Giovanni) was good and dear
and Lily loved him.

But before long, the hand of God
knocked down their front door,
and took away their first born,
and soon after, Zaydeh,
and Ma's best friend and nephew, Davey.
I was born into that chaos and grief,
lingering nameless,
generic *Girl Baby* typed
on my hospital bracelet

this went on for days,
until desperation or embarrassment,
burst loudly into Ma's mind
and she cobbled a name for me
that Uncle Jack refused to pronounce
correctly our whole life together
as uncle and niece
and I couldn't love him—

until I understood
it was his way of making me his own
and loving me out loud
to everyone in the room—
given my own flimsy tether
to my name, which he saw,
and understood.

Hats

Two of my six aunts knitted and smoked,
smoked and knitted through the '50s and '60s.
Clouds swirled round their black bouffants
as they knitted floppy dolls for charity,
and flounce-skirted dolls camouflaging
a toilet paper roll. Ma had no patience for knitting
and couldn't smoke to save her life
though she tried once for her role as a Kit Kat dancer
in *Guys and Dolls* and coughed till she turned green,
but she wore hats like nobody's business
and had a wardrobe shelf
loaded with fancy hatboxes.

Dad loved hats too: his black Russian chapka
and his signature fedora,
two small exotic feathers tucked into its band.
In those days, no self-respecting gentleman
would leave home without a hat.
Fedoras bobbed up and down every avenue
in Manhattan, even in the poorest neighborhoods
heads wore hats, and I don't mean backwards baseball caps.
When a gentleman walked into a building,
even if it was to pay a fine or a loitering bookie,
he removed his hat.

On the top shelf of my disordered closet,
one of Ma's hatboxes survives.
Gossamer tissue enfolds two of her summer hats:
the black straw like the one Audrey Hepburn wore
in *Breakfast at Tiffany's*,
and a traditional boater, black ribbon circling its crown.
I have a big bean-shaped head
and did not inherit Ma's élan in the hat department,
but I knit. Since last July, I've knitted a hat
for everyone I love, and a skein or two for stranger's heads.
I knit on silent circular needles

and can listen to music or cable news
and it gives my hands something to do
because, if I let myself,
I'd chain smoke my way to an early grave.

Nothing Can Stop It

In daylight
        you ignore its vibrations—
                a siren's song

having nothing
        to do with you.
                But the ringing

phone in the night
        shatters glass
               until you wake.

It's turned on
        next to your ear,
                drawing you in

to the surface
        from your deepest dreams
                so fast,

you'll get the bends.
        The ringing phone
                in the night

reaches into your chest
        and squeezes your heart.
                Sleepers stacked

in nearby apartments
        won't hear the ringing
                though they roll over

for a barking dog, crying child.
        At night, the city sleeps,
                but you wake

    from the nightmare
           of the ringing phone,
                  the heavy breathing

    of death's messenger.
           The phone in the night—
                  it has your number.

Two Hawks, Riverside Park

In the photograph of the two hawks,
the male, on the higher limb

of the London plane tree,
has a bloodied shred of a bird

hanging from his beak,
while beneath him

the female
pecks at a rat's carcass

splayed across a lower branch
of that same tree.

The rat's thin black tail
underscores its transformation,

the leafless tree stark
against a cloudy January sky.

I've carried death on my back:
father, mother,

one following the other,
until I'm bent under the weight of it.

I remember as I stood
by the plane tree,

the male stared back,
not eating, while the female

continued to peck,
black tail feathers pointing

at the camera, then seesawing
as her head bent down to tear

and rise up again to eat.
Time, I'm waiting for you.

You do everything swiftly,
but death you do

slow as a swimmer through mud.
I walked on from the tree,

and forgot the dead bird, the rat,
but not the hawks.

Micro-Adjustments

The psoas minor muscles are short,
so to relieve the pain

I shift my pelvis forward,
but my spine's L-5

genetic defect forces me
to shift my sacrum

backward.
I seesaw back and forth:

this way pain,
that way pain.

Well past middle-age
I stand here

and don't know why
I entered this room,

a *tabula rasa,*
then pivot out

into the new-born moment
in which death is no longer

distant. It knocked
on my neighbor's door

just inches from my own,
it squeezed the life

from my ex husband's heart, and the past,
which I thought was tucked up safely

on orderly shelves, burst over me
for imagining once

the two of us finding our way back
to each other as we were.

Travis Is 45

It was a shock
when I did the math
because he was 13
the night my daughter
was born at home.
From the moment he opened
the heavy wooden doors
downstairs, he must have heard
the animal-like utterances
issuing through every crack
and crevice of the old house.
He came running
—was it to save me?—
to the door breathless up
stairs that wound around
to our second floor flat,
his wet hand on the banister.
He came to collect
on the daily paper:
a rag we loved
to search through
to find the hysterical
errors a lazy copy editor
allowed to escape.
—Was he even paid?—
It was a rainy
early November evening,
chilly, but the temperature
in the apartment because
the woodstove was cranked
was close to 90 degrees.
Childbirth is a messy business:
you pace, you climb
up and down stairs, you shit
on newspaper spread
over the floors and you howl—

a knock and your husband opens
the door and there you are—naked
gigantic belly
wriggling forth a baby.

The Body Never Lies

> "…the definition of her six-pack [is] so sharp you could cut yourself on it."
> Courtney Rubin, *NY Times*

The ads in women's magazines
—*Allure, Bust, Curves, Shape*—
are for flat abs and picture young
women whose midriffs announce
the absence of fat, trans
or otherwise.

In their hands
solid black weights,
and on their feet state-of-the-art
trainers in day-glow orange
and pink.

Visceral fat: that roll of flagging flesh
below the shelf of my breasts,
not a concern to these svelte models,
personal trainers and food fetishes aside,

Belly fat—the copy reads—
YOU CAN LOSE IT
IN TIME FOR BIKINI SEASON—
that long-ago time
before 9 months of carrying

the weight of a growing baby
stretched my abdomen with deep
eternal purple radiating
furrows from my belly button
to the bend at my hips.

Naked, before the full-length mirror,
it is Rubens' fleshy women:
Venus, Ceres, and the sleeping Angelica,
I look to now.

A Daughter's Story

We were two adults talking last night,
but I could hear her putting her stamp
on this part of our story.

There is an art to it, the raconteur refining
her timing, compressing her words, sharpening,
not unlike a stand-up comic

holding a microphone as if praying.
I only wish I could have told my mother
what she so easily said to me, her laughter

swaddling the words, so I laughed too.
I didn't know what was coming,
hadn't heard this one before.

When she was four, we sold the house
where she was born, so it was serendipity
years later when she was in high school

that her first boyfriend lived in that house
with his mom who worked long hours.
She lost her virginity in the very room

where she was born, bold exclamation point.
No, I crushed it, adding facts to the narrative.
You were born in the living room.

Your father and I slept in that room,
and I was alone in bed when my water broke
and labor began. Oh gross, Mom, she quailed,

and we both broke up. I could hear her mind
whirring, tossing out that last bit,
revising it right out of her story.

Happy Marriage

I

Guided imagery, she calls it, the young occupational therapist.
New-age music ascends from her phone,
while she strokes my husband's fingers, hand, wrist.

He's in a morphine dream after surviving the surgeon's knife a few days ago
from his breastbone to below his belly button. She draws a finger
through her strawberry blonde hair held precariously back

through devious means I can't fathom,
and works her way up his arm. Traffic on First Avenue is steady:
no pile ups, no horns blaring; I'm studying it,

though I can't make out license plates from this height,
which I would do
to occupy myself and feel invisible.

I'd play that game with myself,
the one we played as kids on boring family drives,
counting up the out-of-town plates:

>   *Massachusetts,* someone yells
>   *I got Rhode Island,*
>   *Ohio,* doubtful,
>   but who'd question it.

This intimacy, the otherworldliness of it
renders a wife superfluous. Behind the billowing
curtain, a man in the opposite bed moans and nurses

in green scrubs and soft-soled shoes scramble
around his bedside I can see under the foreshortened panels.
The pretty OT comes to work in a slim skirt

and V-neck sweater that flatters her figure.
My husband sleeps on,
the faintest smile

on his lips, after teeth-grinding days
of pain I watched, but could work
no magic to alleviate.

II

It's a small 2-man room on the 14th floor for patients moved from the ICU
for observation
that the wife of Bed Number One by the window storms into,
big bag on her shoulder,
big hair teased up, and big make-up glistening
not masking her scowls.
My husband feigns sleep so as not to become collateral damage
in his neighbor's drama
that began playing out with shouting over the phone concerning his release
and her coming to spring him
materialized in the firestorm of her person.
He's a small guy, puny
under a twisted bed sheet, and balding—no doubt, from so much hair pulling.
She's *had it* with him.
She says so, over and over, at full volume. So what, it's a hospital and patients
are recovering
from all manner of serious surgeries—it's the transplant floor—for crying out loud!
But he's *had it* with her too,
he bleats meekly, defensive peacock, though surgery has weakened his fighter
instincts,
which you know he has or their words wouldn't climb to such a pitch
so quickly.
They're pro-wrestlers, forever in the ring, and this is
the *I Love You*
they're most comfortable reminding each other of,
and the world.

III

Later, a blizzard buries us.
My dog's legs are short

and he can't climb the high ridges
the plows pile up. We're wearing

our winter coats: his is navy blue
with an inexplicable pocket,

it can't stop the wind from raging
through anything in its path, yet we stand,

waiting for the light to change.
He shivers in my arms.

*

Each month since fall,
another of my dears

has succumbed to a hospital bed,
tubes and machines tethering each

to a world he or she might leave
without me.

Beeps of a jagged green line
from wires attached to my husband's

chest and arms chart the zigzags
of his breath on a console.

This one means the IV bag is empty.
I hate machines that beep.

*

My dog's legs stick straight out
as I carry him, as if to stave off

the next icy gust.
When his arthritis strikes,

his limbs fold up, and his eyes beseech me.
I hate the clanging radiator,

hot water traveling through its copper course,
and the plow's scraping all night to reach cement.

Elegy I

The loons on East Long Pond went silent
this morning; it's a gray day and the chill
that rolled in from Canada last night

has autumn on its breezy fingertips.
Yesterday, a friend and I spent an hour catching up:
her summer days spent wrapping her mind

around the arthritis in her hands and knees;
my travels, the joys of packing and unpacking.
Our talk circled, an ever-tightening gyre until we arrived at last

upon your name and how abruptly you left us,
disbelief still clanging about our heads. The emails
over your death in the days that followed gave us details,

but no outlet to apprehend, Michael, that you're gone.
We said that's the best way to go, in your sleep
after an evening with friends. We said that's how

we'd like it for ourselves. We said, *so fast*, we never
had a chance to say: what? What would we say?
What *don't* we say to each other every day of our lives

that we now regret not having said to you.
I wrote a note to your wife and son
and told them you always made the weekend coffee

three-times a year when our writers' group met
and how it would be ready when we'd straggle down
in the morning, strong coffee—so strong, we'd complain—

it became a joke, but how could we do without it?
You probably drank a bit that night, smoked
your beloved Marlboros, someone most likely

passed around a joint. It was late by the time you got into bed,
celebrating with friends, other writers
after the young students had gone off excited

to be at Bread Loaf in such heady company.
Was there music—someone's iPod
hooked up to tiny speakers on a table,

maybe a few satisfied dancers? I remember
similar nights in grad school after a day
of good critique, feeling my work, my words

present in my body
and thinking how blessed I was and how
it didn't get any better than this.

Saturday Night at David's or the Right Tool for the Job

It began with the chopping
of fresh dill
and the flat Italian
parsley because
the blade was that sharp
and glided through
the greens.
I was *sous chef*
of dinner. Also,
it was the martini
in a proper long-stemmed
martini glass,
cold gin
with lots of green olives
on an extra long
pick. Four of us
were chefing dinner
for our friends
of long-standing
who chatted loudly
in the living room
and David told his voice
activated music system—
alluringly called
Alexa—
to find Bonnie Raitt.
That's all it took
and we're dancing
around the kitchen island.
I've got a knife
in one hand,
martini in the other:
<u>I'm writing you a love letter</u>
<u>I got the radio on</u>
<u>radio, radio.</u>*

* "Love Letter" Songwriter: Bonnie Hayes, Love Letter lyrics
© Universal Music

WAS HIS

Even before she passed me,
her lead foot on the accelerator,
I saw her neon orange hair
whipping around her head.

Her little black sedan—I don't know—Fiat?
Peugeot?—rapidly gaining car lengths
ahead of me, but not before I read
her license plate:

WAS HIS—the world's shortest novel.
Was hers the world's longest marriage?
He thought she was his—his riding mower
                              his acreage
                              his putter
                              his wife;
and maybe for a while
she thought so too; that was the leg-hold trap
she got free of
and she got the car to boot.

More I hoped: house, furniture,
a fat bank account.
Now she has the pleasure of this
particular revenge: carloads of passing Volvo

station wagons, Ford SUVs and Chevy Minivans
on the roads she travels—today I-89 between
New Hampshire and Vermont, tomorrow,
who knows, I-95 all the way

to Miami Beach—she gives this little gift,
this morsel of gossip, an exercise to jump
start a story, WAS HIS,
and now and forever not, no how, no way.

The Message

Evolved over millennia,
my thumbs, stumpy
and arthritic,
are necessary
for holding onto
my handled cup,
and to sign my name
on a check's
cramped line,
and clumsily tie
my shoelaces,
but the girl—
almost a woman
by the look of her—
metal bolt
in her cheek,
Cyrillic tattoo
on her arm,
streak of purple neon
in her hair—plants her feet
firmly apart on the gritty
subway car floor,
not holding on
to any bar,
so her hands
can wrap around
her smart phone
and her free thumbs
whirl around
the tiny keyboard,
the meaning
of her urgent message
inscrutable on her shining face,
but her thumbs
Oh God,
they scream it.

The #1 Train

Humans unravel in the subway, rush hour bodies in airless heat, coughing, sneezing, the smell of McDonald's fries, luggage on wheels, enormous purses and backpacks, man-spread spilling over seats left and right. A white woman stands in the packed train, clutching an overhead bar, hanging over a black woman sitting next to her small child. The standing woman's cell phone is falling. Several seats down a muscular young black man bobs his head to the sounds in his ear buds. The phone is about to glance off the child's forehead. When it does she will cry out causing the young man to lunge from his seat toward the white woman whose horror in the face of the falling phone is already registering as tears spurt from her eyes that scan faces for anyone who knows her who would vouch that she is not the kind of woman who would intentionally hurt a child, never mind start an incident on the #1 train. The crying woman's tears hit the child's mother's hands just as the sound of her child's cry reaches her ears and her instinct to surround her daughter with her body brings her in contact with the lower body of the woman who is now reaching into her purse extracting a handkerchief she will offer to the child. When he sees the mother accept the handkerchief and begin to daub at her child's cheeks, the young man will sit back down. The little girl stops crying and the woman bends awkwardly to retrieve her cell phone from between so many styles of shoes, sneakers and boots. The subway doors slide open, not fast enough for the one who will fly from the train, and the observers resume their breathing.

Poetry in Motion

Humanity is wedged
into a New York City subway car at rush hour
(which is really any hour)
and there is no need
to hold on, even if you could
reach that nearest silver pole.

The subway could fly sideways
along the tile work and no *body*
would shift, no strand of hair
escape its *do*. No shoe
flirt its way to touch another's shoe.

There's no help for it
if you meet the eyes of a stranger
one too many times.
And the dull signage only reprimands:
Do Not Lean on Door
Riding Between Cars Prohibited
Unlawful to Spit
and catastrophizes

In Case of Fire...
*In Case...*the eye has nowhere to rove.
So I'm transfixed when I spot
a square foot of poetry framed
in a metal holder
under the red dangling
Emergency Pull Brake.

I'm six humans-of-varying-sizes
blocked from the poster
and see only black on white
words shy of the right margin,
a much larger word at the top,
and two small words—*a name?*—
off to the bottom right.

My stop approaches,
but I have to read the poem.
Can't move. Could tip up on my toes
and turn my eyes slightly left
slightly right, but I can't
get to the bottom of it
before I'm expelled.

What Comes After the Middle-Ages?

When the long black hairs tango
in my brush, I have a little funeral
for each one as I tear it
from the bristles and feather
my fingers over the trash can
to let go of the fine little nests.
Some hate to leave me
and hang on through vigorous shaking,
so why didn't they stay on my head?
Sometimes, it is the traitorous
grey-turning-white hairs
that tangle in my brush.

In the photo I keep on my desk
my hair is shockingly black, short and curly.
I hardly remember that other woman.

On lines and in crowds, I study the backs
of gray and white heads
and see pink scalps, and shiny scalps
poking through thin hair.
Is it rational this fear of balding?
Everyone loses
some hair everyday, so says my daughter
of the luxurious auburn locks.
I remove my hat in the subway,
and young men offer me seats.
If it's a long ride, I accept,
though they call me Ma'am.

Elegy II

When I come upon your photo
and remember you're gone
to a place I can't reach
there's a flip in my chest
how can it be
you of all the ones
how could you be gone
your cheeks in the cold
are ruddy red
you wear your pea coat
and navy beret
yours is a whole-body laugh
you drive your black truck
with the Sherpa seat covers
too fast on the highway
we're both anxious
to arrive for years
we've been writers
in a close-knit group
you say 'ony' instead of 'only'
I chop the vegetables
you assemble
the morning frittata
you give savvy advice
because unlike anyone else
I've ever known
your words are bundled
in a flannel of kindness
years ago laid up by a drunk driver
in an ICU your leg shattered
I wrote I combed Vermont
and there wasn't a cannoli
for you to be found
I have this cornucopia
of memories 40 years
of friendship
and I'm thankful for that
but the snow is falling

it's beautiful we'd walk
downtown for sandwiches
we'd buy cream soda
because the store doesn't sell
Dr. Brown's Cel-Ray
and laugh it's such a New York deli thing
I have your stories peopled
with characters who have goodness
in their DNA you birthed them
that way I can't begin to miss you
because the page holds you fast.

Letter in Which Love Is Invoked

Dear One,

Why are the surfaces

of the words *I love you*

thick as pond ice

in January and twice

as impenetrable?

Worse than a *Fireball*

in my mouth,

they burn my tongue.

My reluctant heart's bullseye

throbs with waiting.

Say it,

say *I love you* now.

But I don't and the moment

passes into deeds of loving.

Is it the same, I wonder.

Don't you crave

hearing it spoken?

Are you such a child?

Sure. Once,

I said it often with abandon.

See where that got me.

25 years and half a bed

gone empty; a load of self-pity

to shovel out spoonful by spoonful

takes time.

Words emptied of *I love you*,

take time to fill,

not a gas tank

not a river

not your fault.

It isn't for lack of loving

that I don't say it

to you.

Taking Off from Charles De Gaulle

Taking Off from Charles De Gaulle

For hours the plane sits on the runway
and the pilot, our captain, has run out of apologies.
What began as vague throat-clearing
generalities sung in casual French
comes down to the unvarnished truth:
there is found to be a missing screw
from a panel on a wing, one of many,
not crucial, certainly not enough to ground
an Airbus 777, however, the workers whose job it is
to screw that screw into its housing
are on strike in Paris: *une grève*.
From my window seat, I watch a couple of burly men
heave our baggage, one after another of red
or black rectangles, in a chilly rain onto a belt that disappears
below me into the plane's belly.
They toss with relish especially the soft luggage
onto its zippered faces and I imagine all the hidden
bottles of wine: *beaujoulais, les grands crus*
of *St. Emilion* shattering into liquid layers
in plastic bags swaddled deep between the breasts
of cashmere sweaters, and still the plane
does not move. Now, we've eaten every snack
Air France flight attendants can conjure
from their efficient compartments, soon
we will be on to the dinner trays and after that
le petit dejeuner designated for that hour
they deem morning over Iceland
or Nova Scotia, somewhere where it is still dark
and still night for bleary time-dislocated travelers.
Our captain is sorry, so very sorry in heavily accented English—
he wishes he hadn't taken this flight rotation, wishes
he were still in bed wrapped in his comforter doing what it does best
to comfort him, but no, he is here having to tell us
he must unload the plane after keeping us on board
this airless nodule for 4 hours.
We must deplane because
this bird won't fly.

An Annual Walk

Wind blows our gray hair back from our faces
and not for the first time, my friend's conversation

circles round our age and she asks me, her elder,
though not by much, with her half-smile,

though not entirely in jest, *is life still good after 50?*
She has played the harp for 20 years, the guitar

and dulcimer for many more, and sung her songs
all over the U.S. and Europe since she was a free spirit

in blue jeans earning her keep playing music, teaching yoga
and English wherever she landed.

In our middle age, in springtime Paris where she lives,
we walk along the Seine close to the docked houseboats,

peering into their windows, one sill lined with a flotilla
of rubber ducks. Gray uneven stones beneath our feet,

clear blue-sky overhead and the occasional whiff of piss
under a bridge because nothing is perfect, not even in Paris!

For our *déjeuner*, we eat last night's stir fry
right there on the bank, dangle our feet over its lip,

our impromptu picnic with real silverware,
vegetarian curry, ice-cold water.

The *bateaux mouches* motor down the center of the river and tourists,
enthusiastic in their sun hats and dark glasses,

wave to us. Whoever they decide we are, in that fleeting moment,
they're not even close, and wherever we think they're going next,

we don't have a clue. We wonder—
don't we?—about each other, and about ourselves

in a state of amazed ignorance
that never ages.

Faire la Cuisine

Were you a child
in your family's sunny kitchen
the first time you stood by
and watched your *maman*
or your *grand-mère*
hold over a bowl
of *salade roquette* or *mâche*,
a large spoon into which
she poured *l'huile d'olive*
and *le vinaigre,*
and ferried on the tip
of a smaller spoon,
la moutarde,
mix it all together
in the kingdom
of the spoon
to splash down
over the greens?
In your own pale blue kitchen,
your children stood by you
and watched, and now
your grandchildren
and your great grandchildren watch
as do I,
      unlikeliest friend
      from another continent,
      another culture,
      another generation,
as you dress
our luncheon salad,
with the same *petit geste*
of the wrist,
an economy of movement,
signifying a lifetime
of nothing wasted.

Homage

I've never talked this way; I've never tried, but yesterday,
I met a Chinese poet in Paris who cannot go home. I read out loud
his homage to Allen Ginsberg. I read the name of his country
over and over from his jagged stanzas, his long poem that covers many
pages in a book, his direct address to China who he talks to, croons to,
in tones that rise and fall between bitterness and all its shimmering
opposites.

Someone with orders shot three bullets into Hongbin's father's head
and because this truth stares out from his poems, his country finds him
Undesirable. Once, he flew to China where he and his young daughter
were immediately arrested. Today, he can only talk with his mother by
phone. In his poem, his father's death recurs in the staggering brightness
of a single bulb in a tiny room each time a reader reads it and I am reading it
now.

The door Allen Ginsberg opens for Hongbin bids him welcome to cross
a threshold I have danced upon all my life. Here is anywhere
I wish to travel, so long as I can pay for my ticket and have a passport.
There are few locks that combination won't crack open. I carry
that privilege, though I try to travel light. When I travel I'm uprooted.
I'm a satellite spiraling, yet I travel for pleasure and I can
return.

We say the same words, Hongbin and I: humble, useless, insane,
that reach back and back into how we became who we are
and I wonder where is the intersection of meaning. I wonder
how the words I use mean what he means when he remembers.
I wonder about secrets in his black ink characters, their lines
and swaying figures that describe father, bullet, mother, China,
home.

Soon we will each fly away and for a short time we'll be cradled
by clouds; then each will land at a destination and spend days
consumed by work, and each will have memories that spill
onto paper and memories only a hammer and chisel can pry loose.
I'll think of Hongbin's guarded English peeled of frivolity. I'll listen
to Allen Ginsberg's poems and hear two voices
howl.

Haricots Verts, Belle Mère

At the sink, I snip each tip and tail, a kilo—
    that's a small mountain
        of beans,

not to be confused
    with the string variety
        for these are thin

in their deep green skins
    lanky, in fact. When you say their name
        the "h" is silent.

Why can't we get these in the States?
    my Francophile husband laments
        for the umpteenth time.

He has instructed me on his preferences
    for their preparation,
        and I steam them in a fry pan

with salt, a little water
    and bring them to the table
        crunchy, as they are flavorful

and need no embellishment.
    All my life my fellow humans
        have misspoken my name.

Even as it stared up at them
    from a page—Nadine—they would exclaim!
        You might have found this amusing,

since that is your name, *belle mère* I never knew.
    If you were alive and I
        were the *belle fille* of your dreams,

I'd be your *sous chef*.
    I'd never want to cook without you.
        Into your huge porcelain *cocotte*

go the marinated chicken pieces,
    Spanish olives and prunes.
        I can barely hold its heft

and am reminded
    of how often
        you must have glided it

into your own oven,
    how many dinners you scoured
        from its high sides,

but in the end, it's the *haricots verts*,
    I cut and turn and cut
        that lead me to you,

imagining who you were when you stood
    at your sink, who you might have been
        to me, and I to you.

Expressionism

When Van Gogh painted the woman in the red dress—
      who may have been young,

          but for the garish paint—
          unnaturally thick red lips and rouge pot cheeks,

          who may have been old,
          but for the flatness of her breasts,

          her cinched waist—
          a villainous green turban

          compressing her head—
he did not love his life. No. Maybe

his model didn't love him or her life—
both of them at the end of one or the other.

It's there in the shriek of paint,
not a kind stroke for either of them.

No matter how long you live with it,
it's a surprise.

Many times, I thought to take it down,
remove it altogether,

but the rented flat is more hers than mine
and something about the tilt of her head,

not the fan half furled in her left hand,
not her right arm, elbow jutted out,

wrist barely brushing her waist,
not her one thick brow (the other hidden

by the turban) practically drawn
straight across her face—those rouged cheeks,

none of these, but the beseeching tilt of her head
makes her human.

Synagogues

1

Ma never left the US.
When I tell her where we're traveling next—
China, India, Hungary—she looks as though I said,
"I bought the moon and stars, Ma!"
"Go sit in the synagogues,"
she says, "it will be as if I'm there too."

2

The First Temple stood in Jerusalem
where the 10 tribes of Israel prayed
until they were banished by Nebuchadnezzar II
and the temple razed to the ground:
it was 587 BCE.

3

In 1945, 3,000 Jews were turned away at every port,
then welcomed with nothing but their faith,
to Shanghai. For many years, an elderly Chinese gentleman
has been the caretaker and guide of the compound.
We sit in the sanctuary and he tells their story.
"Each year," he says, "the children, grandchildren
and great grandchildren of those eastern European Jews
returned to the synagogue for a reunion.
Of those 3,000, 7 families are left. *Gavalt!*"
He speaks in combined Yiddish, Chinese, Hebrew and English
with a generous smile and a nod to incongruity.

4

There are 26 Jews living in Cochin, India,
in a place they call *Jew Town,*
and it isn't meant as a slur.
The synagogue is laid out in blue and white tile

with colored glass lanterns dangling
from the ceiling. You can sit on benches
along the sides. There are services once a year
on Rosh Hashanah and Yom Kippur.

5

The synagogue in Budapest is ornate and brightly lit
with shiny wooden pews. The many rows
held the hundreds of Jews who prayed together before March 1944,
when the Nazis invaded Hungary.

6

In an orthodox synagogue in Rome, the men and women sit
mechitzah…separate. The women protected behind a wall
of opaque white muslin. They chant the same prayers,
with the same intensity, but this way there are no distractions.

7

In Venice, the tiny synagogue sits
in one corner of the walled ghetto,
in a small ancient square,
its wooden beams darkened with age.
The tall locked gate is gone now.

8

At her table in Paris, my friend says
after 50 years, she returned to the synagogue
where she was a *Bat Mitzvah*.
She was the first girl in France to stand at the bema and read
that day's portion of the *Torah*.
"When I walked into the sanctuary," she says, "I felt I'd come home."

9
God was already there
when the Baptists bought the synagogue in Cambria Heights.

They kept the stained-glass windows,
bright blue stars of David shining on the heads
of a new congregation.
It was the 70s and barely a minyan gathered:
the old Jews gone to *Hashem,*
the young ones wandering the world.

10

Saturday morning services were long and boring
when I was a fidgety kid in Queens.
I remember mostly old men
in tallisim bobbing from side to side, davening,
a few old women in gaudy veiled hats.
At the Tree of Life Synagogue in Pittsburgh,
it was also a Saturday morning—
October 27, 2018—
the Kohen opened the Ark,
and a gunman opened fire.

Swan Bar

It's Saturday night and we're drinking
a *coup de Champagne* to celebrate
whatever there is left on this planet

to drink to, Daniel who we haven't seen
in over a year and his new love just back from Cannes,
our imminent marriage, and Lionel's historic Swan Bar

in the middle of Montparnasse when suddenly,
Round Midnight's trumpeter goes berserk.
He hasn't played a note, but demands

free beer, and now there are lots of familiar
English four-letter words caroming through the spikey air.
Lionel, frailer than I remember,

straightens himself, throws out his arms
to protect the narrow space between
the swearing musician and a customer he's cursed,

something about Hitler being right
and it's over the top, everyone out of his seat,
every voice taking him on.

When Lionel throws the miscreant out into the street
the few of us who remain climb a couple of stairs
to the back of the club where the upright piano

and microphone have been waiting.
After the sink is emptied and the last glass wiped clean
with her cotton towel, the bar maid

transforms herself into a chanteuse,
and the American piano player improvises
seamless blues, Cole Porter, anything jazzy.

I look over at Lionel and he's still rattled. I wonder
how long can a man last, throwing his no longer young body
at random crazy danger even for the sake of Jazz.

It's close to 2 a.m. and the bar maid is back behind the bar
when we leave. From the car window I see
Lionel's tall shadow in the doorway.

Montparnasse Cemetery

On the holiday of *Toussaint*, the weather
is overcast and cold; the little school

next door is shuttered,
the quartier quiet.

Yellow, crimson, pink
mums for sale

everywhere; homeless men
cocooned in cardboard

in doorways spend no word
on passersby. Late

in the day bells ring out
from the boneyard across the way,

calling back souls who
have been out lollygagging

for hours on benches and leaning
against lamp posts. This time

Sartre sits on Simone's lap.
He giggles, a peal,

and she arches her bushy brows
at the knell, stands abruptly,

but he floats a knowing
smile just above the ground.

Today, anything can happen
and you've opened

your only door
to that possibility.

*Le Béguinage**

They called us *béguines,*
and Lord knows we were beholden
to our benefactors for hearth and home,
but what I remember most of that time
is how different we all were.
People think women in a cloister
are the same: married to God, and caring
little for the outside world.
It makes me laugh now to think of it.
We had our types, some less
contemplative than others, to be sure.
But it wasn't who we were to the outside,
in Brugges, that mattered to me.
It was who we were to each other.
I suppose it's a cliché now
to use the word *sisterhood.*
But then, to live independently,
to close my door,
and hear my own voice in my own head,
to hear silence of my own making,
then to open my door to green grass,
the straight blooming trees
in the courtyard, and all those other
black doors set in their small white dwellings
attached yet separate, encircled
by a high white wall—a wall that kept us
safe. To hear our individual voices
come together in song and prayer
in our little chapel,
a whole assortment of sound:
some deranged to my ear, if I'm honest,
some glorious—I can't tell you
the freedom
to be women with our own commerce.
There were men, yes, workers—
they did the heavy lifting, ha—
but we did our own hammering too

and plenty of it.
They were friendly,
but no, we were beyond
the want of men in our lives.
Can you understand?
We had our own lives,
were responsible for our own selves.
You can't imagine what it meant then,
what women faced outside these walls
everyday under the thumb of fathers, brothers,
husbands, even some sons, God forgive them all.
We got things done—
what do you think—
made decisions collectively,
there was dissent and argument, but
we agreed in the end. Some would be
disgruntled, occasionally,
but it was gotten over, eventually.
Nothing was insurmountable.
Nothing divided us permanently,
except death.

*"*Le Béguinage*": The first *béguinages* were set up in 12th-century France and Belgium. The *beguines* were a religious movement of women who sought to serve God without retiring from the world.

Swans at Ouchy

Swans paddle
near the edge of the harbor
on *Lac Léman*,
their feathers white
as the spiny Alps
surrounding Lausanne.
Colorful boats
line up at anchor;
flags atop masts
snap in the wind:
it's a picture postcard
for sale at the pricey
kiosk. On the slant
of cement boat launch,
the one with the oil slick
on its back stands,
its neck and head twisted
round its side.
To get at its hurt
the swan gnaws
and pecks itself.
One unlucky swan—
not such a blight
on an otherwise
pristine view
where tourists troll
the waterfront in blissful
ignorance of one creature
doomed in the harbor.
I wish I hadn't seen it—
could have seen it anywhere—
Manhattan, on the Hudson,
no swans, a man
sleeping on a grate.

Hvar Panorama

Begin from the bougainvillea Marica's been tending for 29-years,
reaching up and over the second story balcony: magenta spade-shaped petals,
a scattering of yellow circles—pistils—among the stick brown stamens:
a fat black bee languorously bumbling from one cluster to another.

Opposite, low two-storied buildings, tiered red tiled roofs built close
climb the hillside where a woman on a far balcony hangs bedsheets
the size of postage stamps: pale yellow, pale pink, pale purple—the only activity—
the rest still as a postcard. Above them, rocky tree-laced peaks, then panning left,

an opening out, the sea dotted with boats of all sizes: dinghies, skiffs, sunfishes,
fishing boats, water taxis, yachts, an ocean liner with four stacks dwarfing
the small U-shaped harbor, fewer and fewer boats the farther the eye travels,
until a clear swath of cerulean blue water reaches the horizon.

The circle complete, you return to where you began on Marica's balcony,
bougainvillea branches cascading to rest on the red tile floor. Painted toes
on slender tanned feet tucked under a small oilcloth covered table:
a ripe peach on a plate atop the shaded table, a knife laid by, no, a pen, my hand.

Taste, Memory

The drive between Sevilla and Cordoba,
Cordoba and Granada, Granada and Nerja
on the smaller roads, designated "D" and barely
visible on the *Michelin* map of Spain,

becomes more windy and hillier, high Sierra peaks fill in
the backdrop. The contrast between green hills and snowy
mountains beyond, under a sun-blue sky is enough,
but then, as if painted in perfectly straight rows

that wrap themselves around and around, up one side
and down another, hand-planted mature olive trees,
and the aroma saturating the air on a crisp January morning
hits me in the face when I crack open the car window.

Eventually, my eyes and nose conspire to awaken
my taste buds, and I crave olive oil.
Everyone who lives here must crave olive oil.
Every morning we order tostada, and a glass bottle

of local olive oil, another of whole garlic cloves floating
in oil, and one of fresh pureed tomatoes arrive at our table.
It is as though we've never breakfasted before.
Through a clear glass bottle, the color

is the green of dusty trees in open air, green of late
summer through a transparent curtain. The taste is of olive
and pit, leaf and tree, soil and rain, the hands that pick the fruit.
We vow to eat tostada and olive oil for breakfasts ever more.

We buy the local oil and carry it home in our suitcases
as though it is contraband, as though everything else
in the suitcase serves to buffer and protect it
on its journey. Nothing has ever held me in such thrall

as does the green liquid dream that soon
taxes my greed of a memory we can but share.
At home, we watch the level in the bottle
diminish meal after meal, and I worry.

Voyage Out

No one is on the beach at this hour
before sunset in Izmir.

The restaurants are shuttered between seasons.
There are no Cinzano umbrellas,

and no soft cushions on rattan loungers.
The palms stand alone, but the sky

is full of biblical drama
in blazes of purple and gold.

We're traveling in Turkey,
our first trip together in a long friendship.

The wind whips sand around my ankles
in tiny pin pricks.

I hold the huge bath towel around her tall figure,
as she changes into her bathing suit,

and she does the same for me.
Naked for that moment in such a country

feels dangerous and delicious,
but I'm too cautious even to wade into the sea.

She steps fearlessly
into the frigid water,

plunges in, swimming back and forth
beyond breaking waves.

I edge the water,
watch her take on the Aegean.

Now & Then

Even then, in 2005, we were warned
not to travel east to Ankara,
but Istanbul was still safe for two women
traveling unaccompanied,
two friends sailing down the Bosporus.
The changes were happening slowly,
happening as we walked along
with women in blue or black burkas,
and tourists in shorts and sneakers,
their cameras bobbing over protruding bellies
through the bazaar. No one took notice of us
in our tank tops and long skirts.
At the Blue Mosque, covered down to our ankles,
our heads swathed in yards of fabric,
it was an old woman who spotted my wrist
poking out of my blue-sleeved blouse.
She tapped it hard several times
and scolded in angry Turkish
to let me know my offence.
Ten years after the photograph was taken—
a sliver of moon
above a blurred water taxi's lit decks—
the image labeled
Nadell's Evening on the Bosporus
pops up on my computer screen.
We might have travelled to a distant planet
for how little freedom resides there now.
It *was* my evening, newly single
and traveling farther
than I'd ever been before.

Why She Falls

That day, many sick people blew their noses.
There was the man on the other side of the café glass
pacing and blowing, so she wasn't the only one
with a crumpled Kleenex in hand,
though she was the one who flayed her body
along the wretched cobbles that grabbed her shoe
and sent her flying in front of the Russian Embassy
on *Unter den Linden Strasse* in Berlin
that autumn afternoon.
No one approached until a peevish guard
who was annoyed perhaps,
by the obstacle she presented to his watch,
helped her lift herself
and quickly returned to the other guard
at their post as she limped away, embarrassed.
She'd stopped counting since the fall before,
when she crossed *Boulevard Raspail* in Paris
in her winter coat, the last snap binding her calves,
restricting her stride as she stepped into the crosswalk
for what she thought would be an easy run against traffic
that looked far enough away
until instinctively she threw out her arms
to stave off the asphalt that reared up at her.
She cringed and turned her face
away from the distant *Grube* truck and motorcycle she'd seen
before she fell and that were now bearing down on her.
Seven falls in six years. This new trip up was a setback
though maybe falling is nothing but the body letting go,
the thrill of weightlessness, kin to the risk of falling
in love. She thought she was through with all that
and now there was this fresh cut on her palm,
beginning again.

Moscow: Fear & Trembling

It began with a bee on the bus. It sat there on the fleshy part
of my hand as if invited: a bumblebee the size of a U.S. half dollar,
yellow and black stripes, long bent hairy legs.

The slightest pressure caused me to look down then—
how long had it been there—I flicked my hand reflexively;
out of fear. It landed on the window next to me.

A young man on the aisle was watching.
He came and cupped it in his hands, let it rest there.
I left the bus trembling. It was a sunny day

and tourists, including me, were out in numbers.
Another stop on the tour: the new Olympic Stadium
on one side of the vast road;

Moscow University, *tallest educational building in the world;*
and many plush-seated buses lining up at the curb.
Then I noticed a peculiar choreography between a thin Chinese woman

and a young man with two white cockatiels perched on his arms.
I had seen this man earlier on Arbat Street, near our hotel.
The birds were props in a scam, but you don't know it

until he inveigles you to clip a bird or two on your arm:
"Wouldn't you like a photograph taken of yourself with these brilliant
white birds, of course you would, what a souvenir, such beautiful birds,

so well trained, they never fly away." Then,
when he takes the birds back, you have to pay, but the woman
did not know this, and now the man and his birds

stalked her: every time she moved, he moved.
Her face said she was confused, terrified. Her face said *Help Me,*
though she spoke softly in her language.

I watched for longer than I should have, until I understood.
I left my huddle of safety and walked the few yards
to where they two-stepped, the birds between them,

and put my arm around her. "There you are," I said, "you have to go,
your friends are waiting for you!" And indeed, they were standing by
the curb, not knowing what to do. He objected loudly in Russian.

We couldn't shake him. Then I stopped, looked him in the eyes:
"NO. Stop It Now," I shouted in his face and stunned him.
He stopped moving and I scooted her away to her friends.

She thanked me in whispers. It happened quickly
before it caused a commotion, though he continued to protest
to anyone who would listen. I returned to the bus, trembling.

Road Trip

In the back seat of the red rented Renault
G and I bump along, husbands up front;
they switch back and forth from driver
to navigator. They've known each other
since they were 15 when they met
at École Alsacienne.

Off the paved road
the dirt turns to mud, turns to chickens
and goats, turns to dead ends
and we're backtracking to regain our route
in the lush Cuban countryside.

We pass billboards of Che's visage,
PATRIA O MUERTE and VIVA FIDEL.
When we spot Presidente Raul's message:
Sí se pudo, Sí se puede, Sí se podrá,
the four of us talk at the same time.

How do political slogans
translate to the feeling
Cuba is my homeland,
which we hear in the warmth
of the Cubans we talk with
over many dishes of rice and beans?

Also, we are lost with spotty GPS
and limited cell phone service.

Over the past years, G's English has improved
after watching Hollywood films on French TV
with subtitles, while my French falters with disuse.
Together, we land in Spanish, both having studied it
in school. There, in words long ago lived for me
on the pages of textbooks, we converse in simple phrases
and sentences in the present tense where they are alive
in our mouths.

Unfolding ourselves out of the car,
we walk arm in arm, or hold hands
happy to be friends in any language.

Coda

Lady's Slipper

If there were a creator
of the universe, and if she
were to begin again,
having deemed the first draft,
if not a failure,
then in need of serious revision—
after light cracked its shell
open against the sky,
water trickled
then cascaded
from every promontory,
air breezed over forest tops
and oceans—when she got down
to the minutiae—
and the architecture
of a new being
and new knowledge—
there would be many do-overs—
the apple's reputation
resurrected apart from the snake—
and many successes to repeat
in nature, and above all,
she would know the Lady's Slipper
to be among her most perfect designs
and from its pale pink
swelling sides,
as they curve inward
on their veined way
toward a secret center,
she would know it to be
the template
for that part
of a woman's body
in which coexist her pleasure
and her pain.

NOTES:

"Elegy I" is in memory of Michael Macklin.

"Saturday Night at David's or the Right Tool for the Job" is for Erika, Bill and David. "Love Letter" Songwriter: Bonnie Hayes, Love Letter lyrics © Universal Music

"Elegy II" is for Bill Gazzola.

"An Annual Walk" is for Lisa Morrison.

"Faire la Cuisine" is in memory of Nicole Alby.

"Haricots Verts, Belle Mère" is in memory of Nadine Rodwin.

"Swan Bar" is for Lionel Bloom, owner of the former Swan Bar of Montparnasse in Paris.

"Le Béguinage": The first *béguinages* were set up in 12th-century France and Belgium. The *béguines* were a religious movement of women who sought to serve God without retiring from the world.

"Road Trip" is for Guylaine Senechal.

Nadell Fishman published two previous collections of poems: *Drive*, Brown Pepper Press, 2001, and *At Work in the Bridal Industry,* Plain View Press, 2011. Ms Fishman taught writing, literature, and women's studies at Vermont College for more than 20 years. For the last 15 years she has travelled extensively throughout Europe and Asia. She lives in central Vermont with her husband and their dog, Kasha.

www.ingramcontent.com/pod-product-compliance
Lightning Source LLC
Chambersburg PA
CBHW030224170426
43194CB00007BA/849